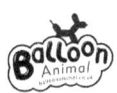

Six Packet Cuts

First published in Great Britain in 2024 by Balloon Animal

Text copyright © 2024 David Crofts

Illustrations copyright © 2024 David Crofts

The right of David Crofts to be identified as the author and illustrator of this work has been asserted.

All rights reserved. No part of this publication may be reproduced, stored in or introduced to a retrieval system or transmitted in any form or by any means (electronic, mechanical, photocopying, recording or otherwise) without the prior written permission of the publisher.

A CIP record for this title is available from the British Library

ISBN 978-1-7396081-2-5

1 3 5 7 9 10 8 6 4 2

Six Packet Cuts

6 Packet Hinge Cut

and

6 Packet Display Cut

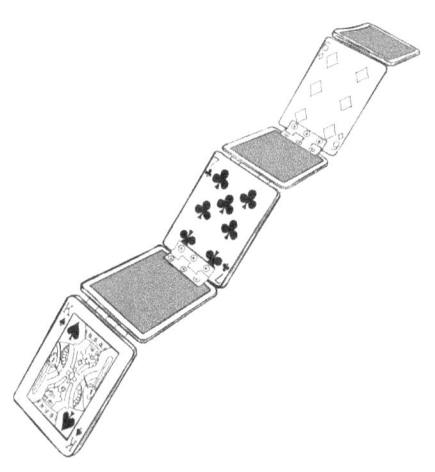

Created, written and illustrated by David Crofts

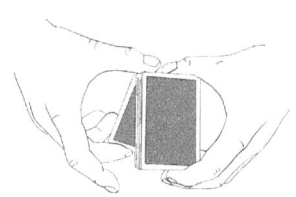 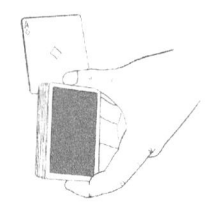 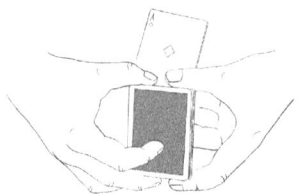

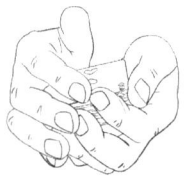

Overview

Clockwise from top left...

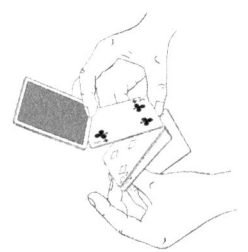

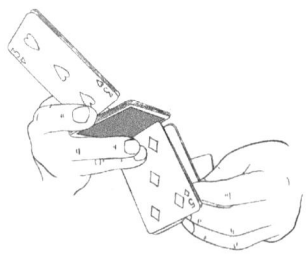

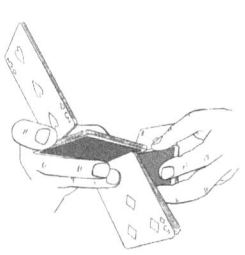

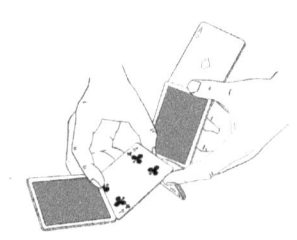

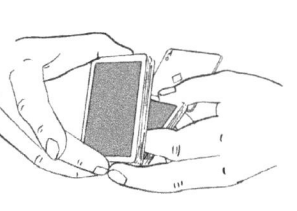 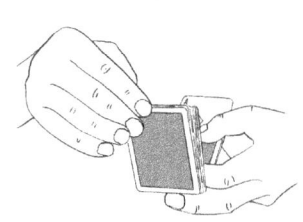 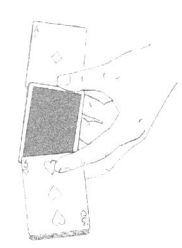

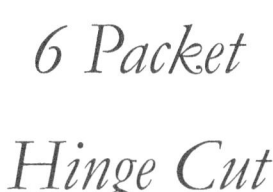

6 Packet
Hinge Cut

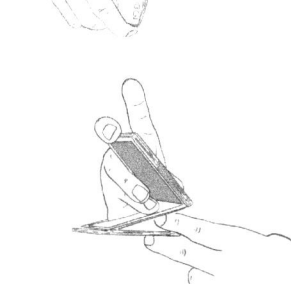

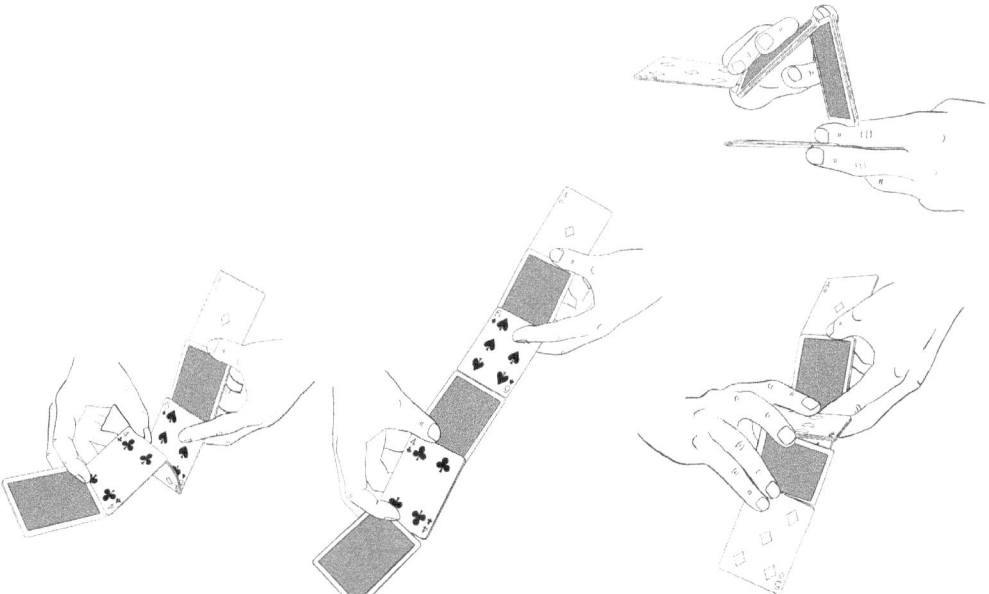

6 Packet Hinge Cut

The pack is held face down between the hands from above with the thumbs at the inner short end and the left 1st finger and right 2nd finger at the outer short end. From the bottom of the pack, a small packet is broken off by the right 2nd finger and hinged back by the right 2nd finger and thumb. The packet hinges at the inner short edge at the thumbs. The right hand turns palm up, hinging this packet face up. This face up section, once it is in line with the rest of the pack, is gripped between the left thumb above and left 4th finger below as in the second picture below.

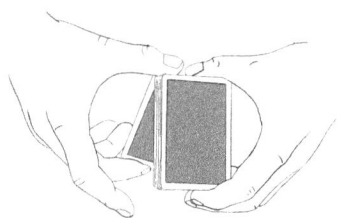 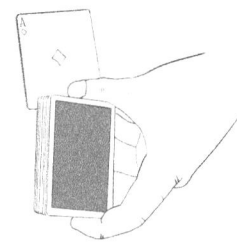

The right hand is now free to re-grip the face down section of the pack with the right thumb near the left thumb and the right 2nd and 3rd fingers near the left 1st finger at the outer short edge. The right 1st finger rests lightly on the top of this face down section. The right thumb breaks off another packet and begins to hinge it upwards, hinging it at the outer end, at the left 1st finger and right 2nd finger. As this third section is hinged up, the outer end of the face down packet is transferred from the left 1st finger to the left 2nd finger. The left 1st finger is free to move into the 'V' shaped gap between the second and third sections, as in the second picture below.

Note that the packet just broken off and hinging upwards is a larger packet which will subsequently be split into four more packets.

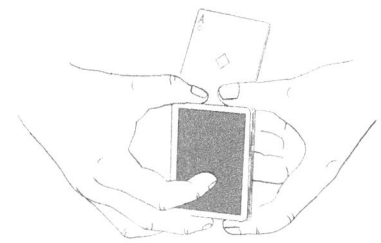 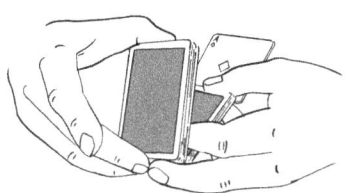

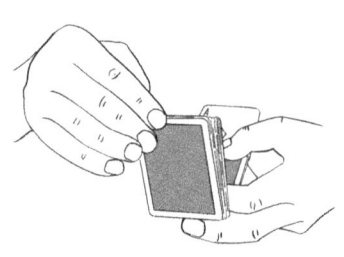

The right 1st and 2nd fingers slide up the back of this new third section towards the right thumb. This third packet is now gripped between the right thumb and right 1st and 2nd fingers at the outer short end, and remains in contact with the left 1st and 2nd fingers at the hinge.

The packet is hinged out flat and in line with the first two sections and is clipped at the hinge between the left 1st and 2nd fingers. The right hand is once again free.

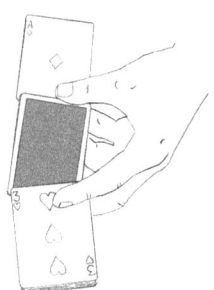

The right hand re-grips the outer face up section from above, between the right 2nd and 3rd fingers at the outer short edge, and the right thumb at the inner short edge. The right 1st finger curls on top. The left 1st finger releases its grip on the top of this section, allowing the right thumb to riffle up the cards at the inner short edge at the corner and to make a break in this face up packet. The left 1st finger bends and then straightens entering into the break. The left 1st and 2nd fingers re-clip the lower part of this third section.

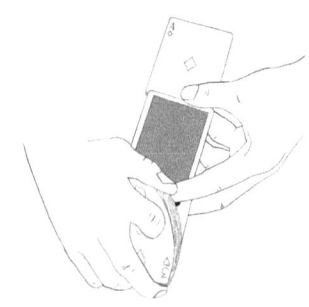

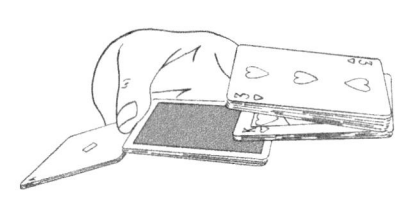

The upper section of this outermost packet can be left momentarily resting on the lower section; resting on the lower section at its outer end and on the left 1st finger at its inner end, the two sections being kept separate by the left 1st finger. The right hand is now theoretically free...

...but although this resting position is held for almost no time at all, while the right hand moves into its next position, the cards do need to be held more or less horizontally to help secure the upper packet in place and to prevent it from sliding away. With a line of three packets in place, the remaining three packets of the six packet hinge cut will be hinged out from the packet which is resting on top.

This balancing section is gripped between the right 2nd finger at the outer short edge and the right thumb at the inner short edge. The right 2nd finger makes a break and lifts up about two thirds of this packet, the right thumb acting as the hinge.

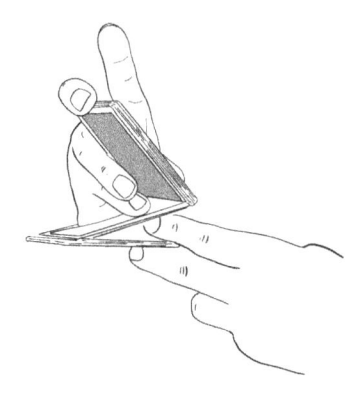

The right 3rd and 4th finger enter the 'V' shaped gap between the two parts of the split packet. The lower section of this split packet is gripped between the right 4th finger and the right thumb, near the hinge. The upper section is gripped between the right 2nd finger at the outer short end and the right thumb at the inner short end, again near the hinge. Note that at this point the hands could be parted, three sections in the left and two sections in the right. The cards could also be opened out into a five packets, as in the picture to the right, but rather than this they are kept in place in position, as in the previous picture, ready for the sixth packet to be hinged open.

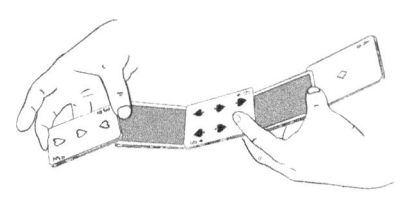

The short edge of the fifth section, at the hinge, makes contact with the side of the left 1st finger. This will happen naturally about halfway between the middle and tip of the finger, as in the picture to the right. The sixth section hinges out between the side of the left 1st finger and the tip of the right 2nd finger. Note that in these pictures the first two packets are hidden behind the left hand.

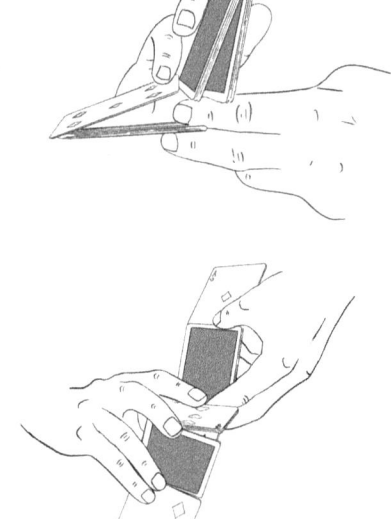

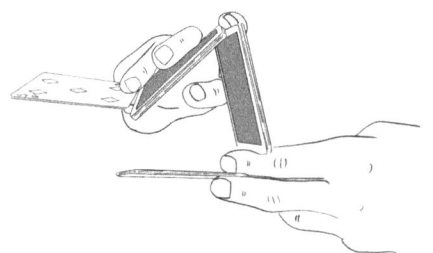

Also note that for a brief moment the integrity of the chain is broken at the far end as the hinge between the first three packets and the final three packets slightly separate, as in the pictures above. This happens so briefly that it does not spoil the overall effect. However, as a variation, it is possible to lift up the whole arrangement in front of the face and to open up this last section at the left side corner by the hinge, with the right side tip of the nose, instead of the side of the left 1st finger, while keeping all the packets more or less correctly aligned.

The right 1st finger bends and then straightens, entering the 'V' shaped gap between the fifth and sixth sections. The sixth section is clipped between the right 1st and 2nd fingers. There are now three sections held independently in each hand and the hands are free to move apart displaying two separate three packet hinge cuts.

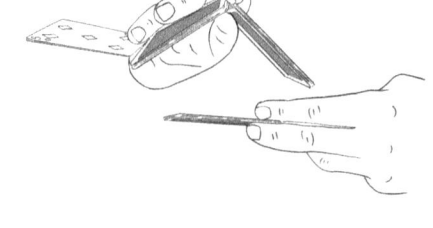

But what actually happens is that...

The right hand immediately rotates clockwise, turning palm up, and turning its whole set of three packets over so that the far packet turns face down and becomes the joining packet, joining onto the left hand's outer face up packet. The pair of three section sets, are positioned in line with each other, with the right hand in front, restoring the appearance of the folded out chain.

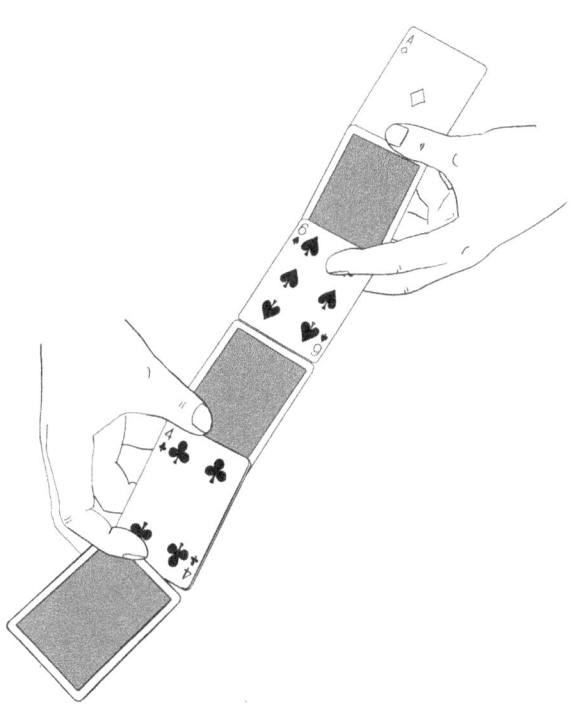

Note that it is the packet clipped between the right 4th finger and thumb which is held as if connected to the packet clipped between the left 1st and 2nd fingers. In other words, the five of diamonds in the previous pictures turns face down and connects with the face up six of spades.

Fantastic, well done, you've made it this far. Thank you for following along so nicely! The 6 packet hinge cut can be displayed horizontally or vertically, lifted up to the face, with a big cheesy smile (or not) being careful to keep the two sets of three packets as if connected. Alternatively it can be opened and immediately closed in one continuous, fluid action, with little or no pause.

The right hand begins to turn back palm down, rotating anti-clockwise so that a 'V' shape gap forms between the two middle sections of the chain, between the third and forth sections. These two middle packets are the first packets to be joined together and closed.

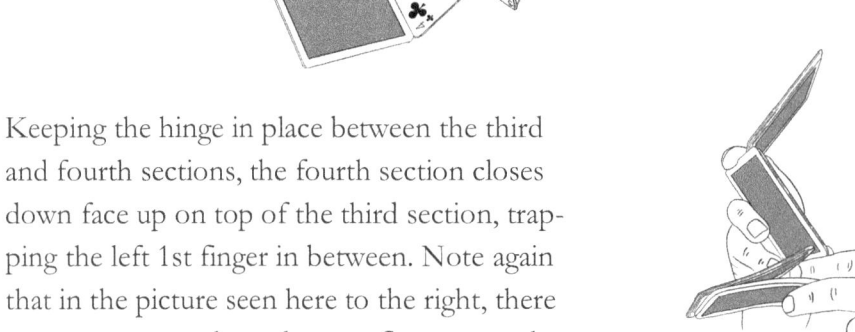

Keeping the hinge in place between the third and fourth sections, the fourth section closes down face up on top of the third section, trapping the left 1st finger in between. Note again that in the picture seen here to the right, there are two more packets, the very first two packets, which are hidden behind the left hand.

The left 1st finger is removed from between the two aligned packets, allowing the two packets to join, leaving this new double section momentarily clipped between the tip of the left 2nd finger from below and the tip of the right 4th finger above as in the first picture below.

Note, again, in this picture, there are two packets, the very first two packets, hidden behind the left hand.

The right thumb joins and then takes the place of the left 2nd finger on the back of this double packet, as in the second picture below.

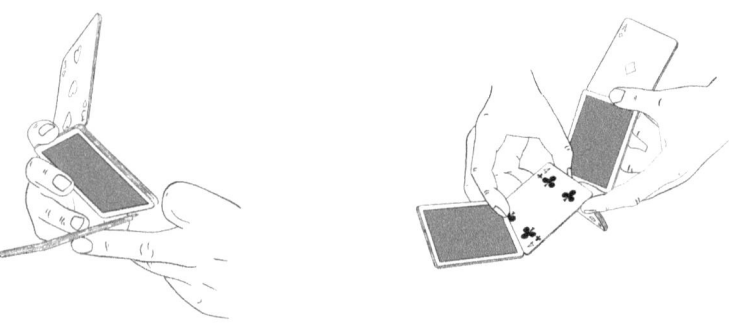

The right hand is again now in control of three packets, while the left hand is in control of just two.

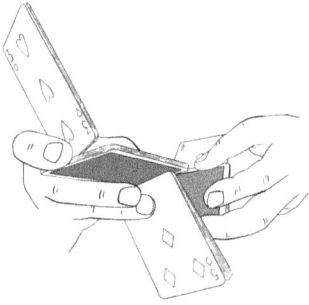

The left 2nd finger moves from the outer short end of its face down packet to further in along the face of this outer face down packet and presses upwards on the face of this packet from below. This starts to hinge the left hand's two packets closed, as in the first picture below.

The back of the lower packet of the right hand's chain of three packets, aligns against the left hand's outer packet, further pressing the left hand's packets closed, as in the second picture below.

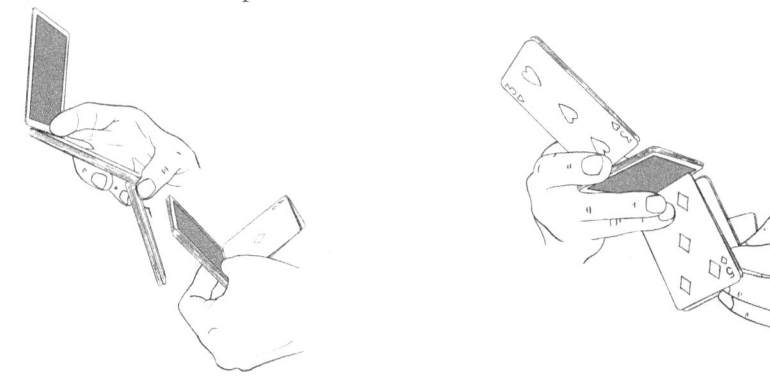

The left hand's two packets are closed with the left thumb being trapped between them.

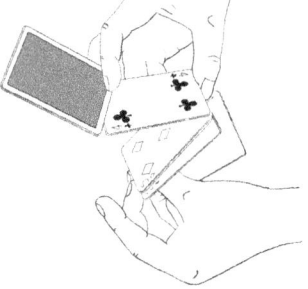

13

The right thumb moves to the back of this now triple packet, with the right hand becoming again in control of three packets. But now, only one packet remains in the left hand, the first packet which had been hinged out from the original bottom of the pack right at the start of the cut.

This left hand's remaining packet is still being clipped at its outer short end between the left thumb from above and the left 4th finger from below.

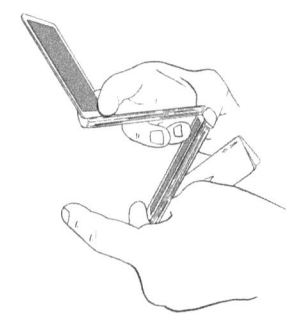

The big triple packet is hinged down and closed on top of the left hand's one remaining packet, with the left thumb being trapped in between.

The triple packet rests on the left hand's section whilst still being gripped between the right thumb and 4th finger. It is also aligned in place by the left 2nd finger at its outer end. The next packet is still gripped between the right thumb at the inner short end and the right 2nd finger at the outer short end. The final face up upper section is still clipped between the right 1st and 2nd fingers. The right hand further hinges its three packets closed, lowering the fifth section down onto the cards below, with the right 3rd and 4th fingers trapped in between. The right 1st and 2nd fingers relax their grip on the sixth section allowing it to tilt down horizontally, aligning and hinging down on top of the rest of the cards below.

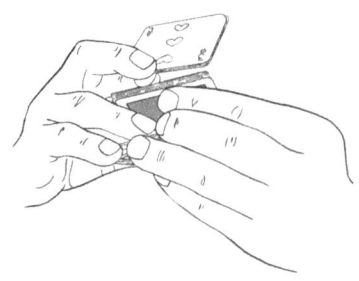 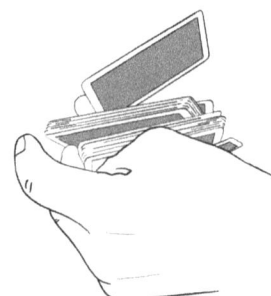

The left thumb and the right 1st, 3rd and 4th fingers being trapped between the packets are removed as the pack is squared up by the left hand from below and by the right hand from the right side and from above.

Well done for getting to this point - a lot of words and a lot of pictures to describe many small actions all of which blend smoothly together creating one big action - the six packet hinge cut.

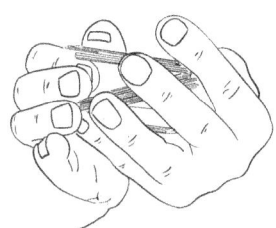 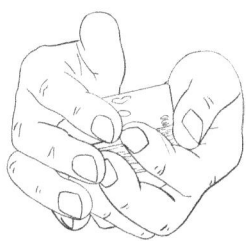

If the pack begins face down, as in the instructions here, after the six packet hinge cut is complete the entire pack finishes off… face up.

Combined with other hinge cuts, the two packet, three packet, the four and five packet hinge cuts, as explained in the 'The Hinged Deck', a routine can be created out of these cuts.

It's a long card flourish to describe and can be quick or long to perform depending on style and speed, and it's also long in shape, over a foot and half long. Using bridge size cards, which are slightly narrower than standard poker size cards the physical length of the cut is accentuated, especially when contrasted with the a six packet hinge cut with the cards held sideways. No description is needed for the sideways six packet cut; it's the same handling as the six packet hinge cut here, but with the cards held sideways.

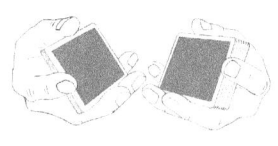 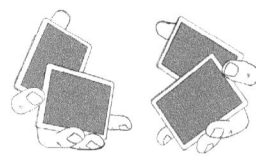 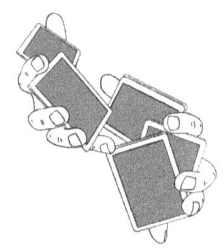

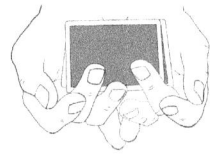

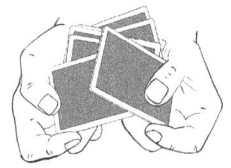

Overview

Clockwise from top left...

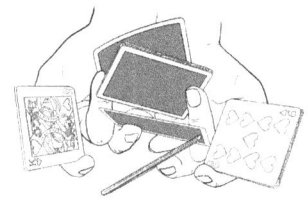

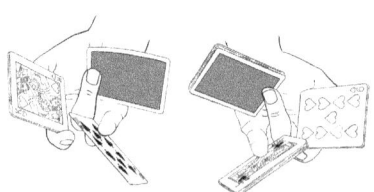

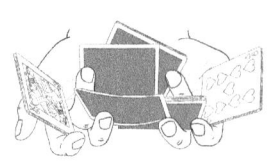 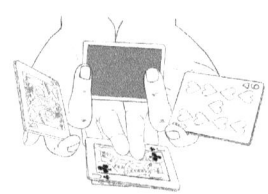 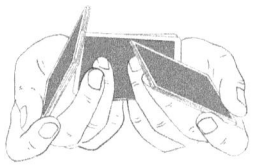

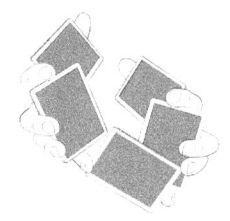 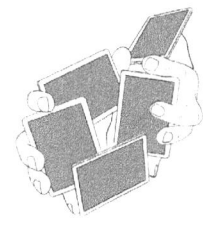 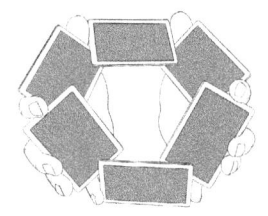

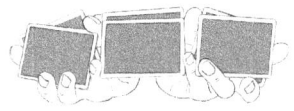

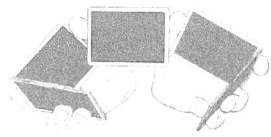

6 Packet
Display Cut

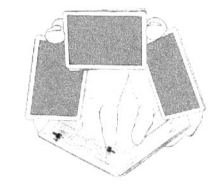

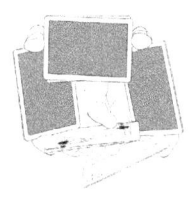

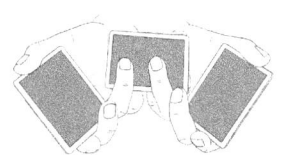 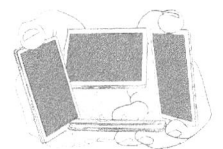 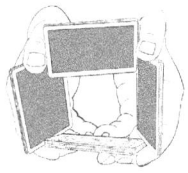

6 Packet Display Cut

The pack is held in the left hand with the left 1st finger curled underneath. The thumb riffles off about a third of the cards at the outer left corner and enters into the break pushing this smaller packet upwards and over, so that it lands face up on the left and right fingers.

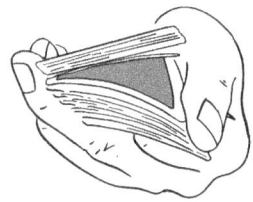 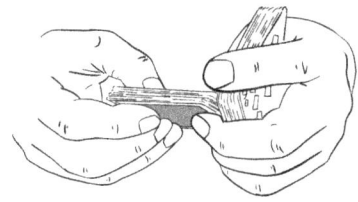

The left fingers continue pushing up underneath the left long side of this face up packet, pushing it up and over, so that it continues rolling over, turning and landing face down in the right hand. This is a similar action to the standard way of splitting the pack for an in the hands riffle shuffle but with the cards held sideways.

The packets are then raised into a higher grip as if getting ready for Charlier cuts. The 1st and 4th fingers are at opposite short sides and the thumbs, and 2nd and 3rd fingers are at opposite long sides.

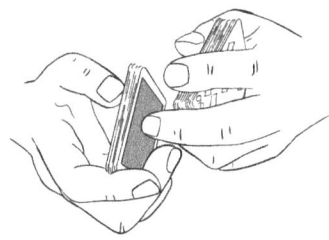 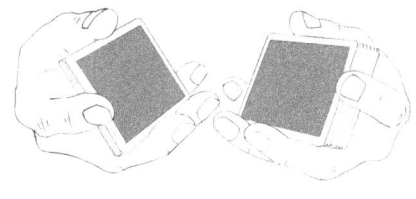

The thumbs contact the inner short ends, at the corners above the 4th fingers, and break off the bottom half of these packets, pivoting the packets against the 1st fingers.

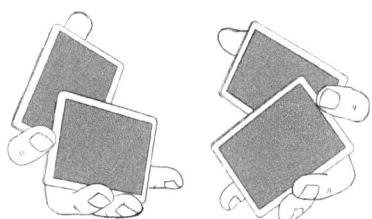

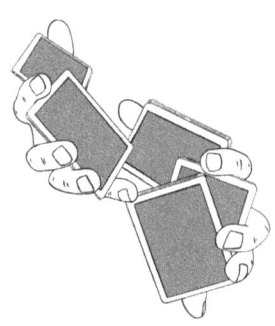 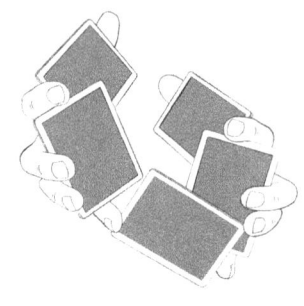

At this early point in the cut, two scissor cuts could be performed as described on page 29.

However, instead of scissor cuts, what actually happens next is that the tip of the right 4th finger makes contact with the left hand's outer packet, to the right of the left 1st finger-tip. This packet is split in half, the right 4th finger pivoting half the packet away, pivoting the packet against the left 4th finger, as in the two pictures above.

At this point the two hands could be further separated to make a nice stretched out five packet display as below, with all the actions then being reversed and the pack squared up. Alternatively, the thumbs could move together to make a pentagon display, as in the second picture below.

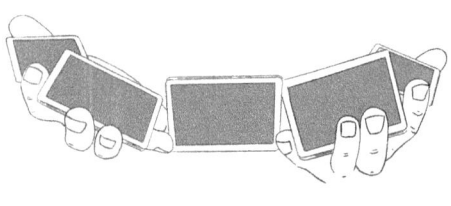 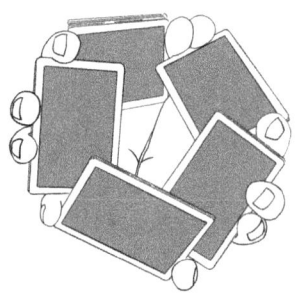

But don't be distracted, diverted, deviated or disillusioned by these possibilities as what actually happens is that...

The back of the right thumb makes contact with the short edge of the left hand's other packet, that is, the packet held between the left thumb and 1st finger, making contact to the right of the left 1st finger.

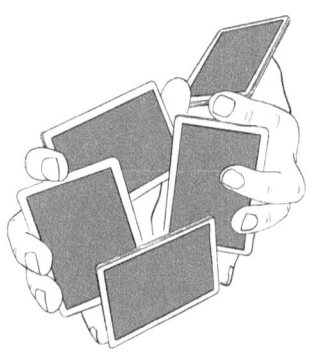

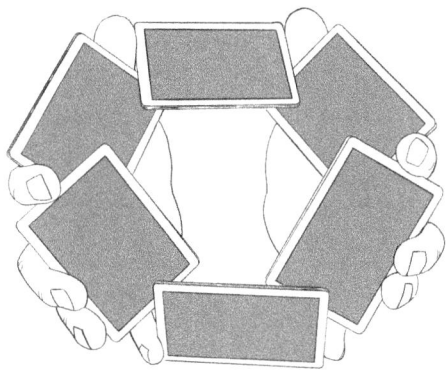

This packet is then split in half, the right thumb pivoting half the packet away, pivoting the packet against the left thumb resulting in six packets being opened out into a circle or rather a hexagon. This is really the starting point of the cut and all the displays to follow. Rotate the hands. Flex it, squish it, squash it. Maybe not too much … as this might result in the 52 card pick up.

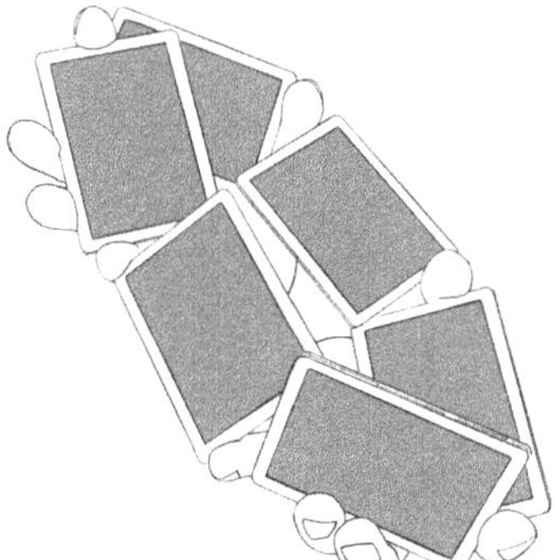

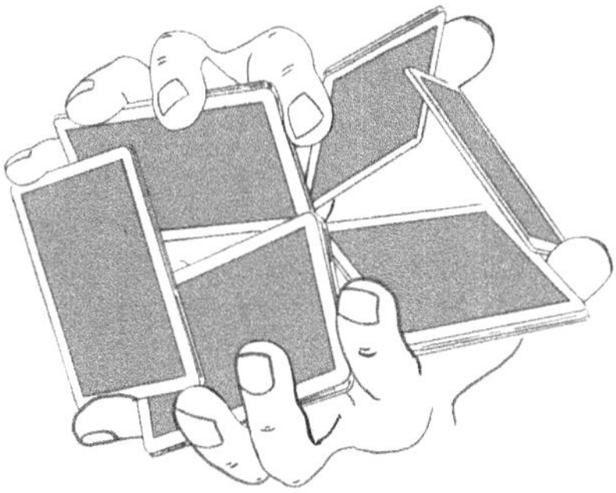

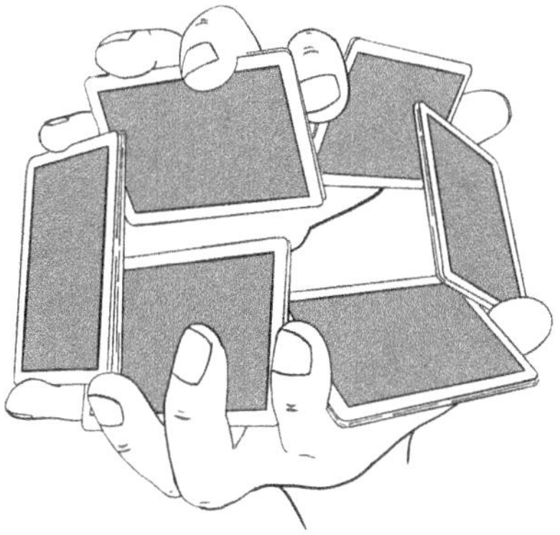

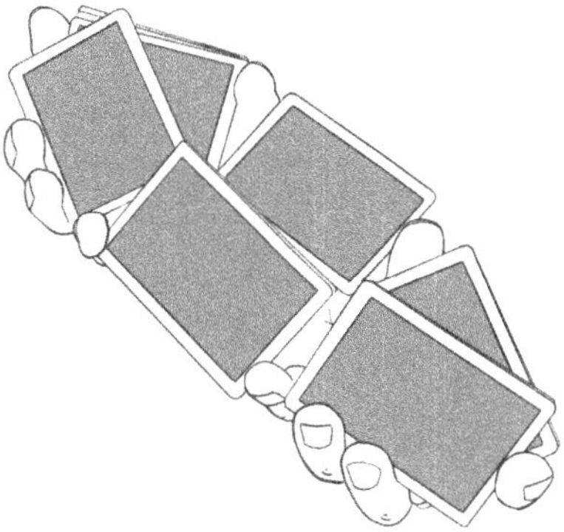

The first phase is complete; only another six phases to go and all that squishing and squashing on the previous page will really help, refining the grips, getting prepared and limbered up for what is to follow.

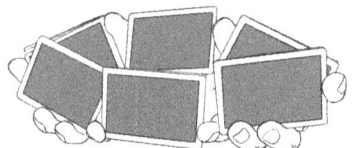 The right thumb and right 4th finger move towards each other. The left thumb and left 4th finger also move together. The middle packet held between the thumbs lowers behind the middle packet held between the 4th fingers.

In a similar way, the packets on either side held between the thumbs and 1st fingers move behind the packets held between the thumbs and 4th fingers.

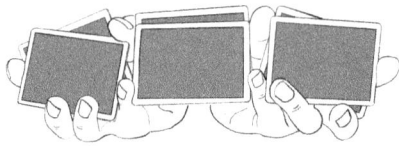

The middle packets are aligned and join, and are re-gripped as one, with the back of a thumb on both short sides.

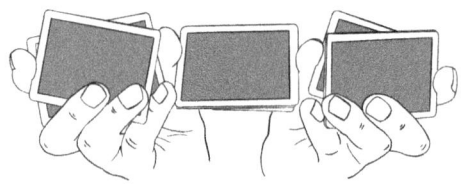

If seated or at a table, the middle packets can be given a little tap on the table, along the lower long edge, to help align them, the side packets being pivoted slightly upwards and out of the way, as in the picture to the right.

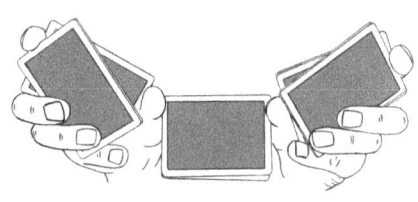

It is possible to join the side packets as well, making a three packet line which can then be zig zagged closed in a number of ways, as in the three packet close variations starting on page 30, but although, at a glance, the line of cards resembles three packets in a row… it is still really five packets and it is now time to open it up again … back into five packets.

The right 3rd and 4th fingers move away from the right thumb, as do the left 3rd and 4th fingers, moving away from the left thumb. The 4th fingers slide round from the corners of their packets to the faces of their packets, with the back of the 4th finger nails pressing on the faces. The 2nd and 3rd fingers also slide to a more central position behind the backs of their packets.

The hands can be brought together creating a new five packet circle, as in the second picture below. Notice how it contrasts with the earlier flat pentagon.

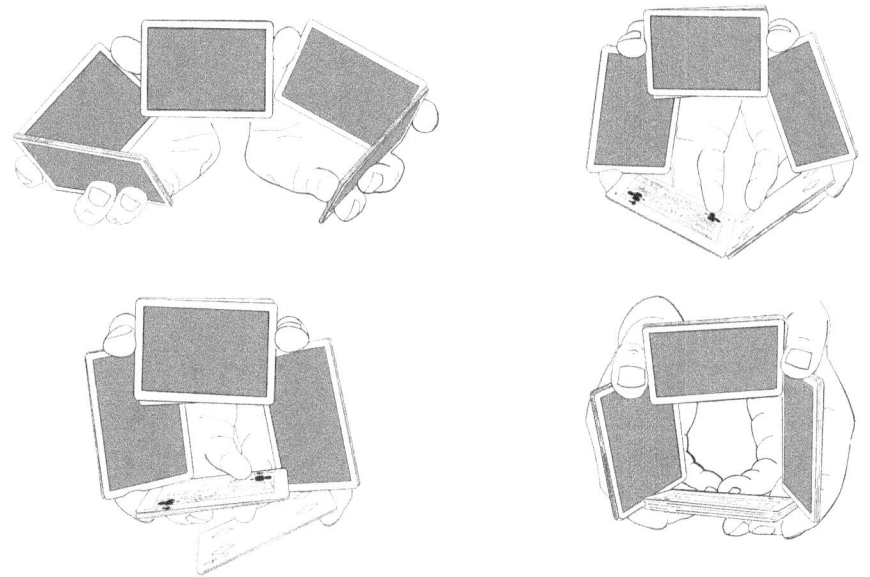

We are ready for the packets to be arranged into a more solid four packet square. For a faster and smoother cut, the five packet pentagon above can be missed out, by continuing straight into the following four packet display.

The lowermost packet held in the right hand between the right 4th finger and 2nd and 3rd fingers is moved in above the lowermost packet in the left hand.

The left 4th finger momentarily lifts up as the right hand's packet is slid underneath it. The right 2nd and 3rd fingers slide behind the left hand's lowermost packet as the two packets are aligned and join together as one. This process can be seen in the two pictures directly above.

It might not look as if much has happened between the last picture on the previous page and the first picture below but a closer look will reveal that the packet which was clipped between the thumbs has been allowed to fall. The thumbs move apart dropping this packet and allowing it to fall onto the palms, resting between the two hands. If the hands are tilted back towards the body this can help ensure the packet falls face down. Alternatively, the packet can fall face up, as in the second picture below and the 4th fingers can kick it back over face down. At this point, the hands can also squeeze slightly together to gently clip this packet between the palms, allowing both hands to tilt forward for a more open display.

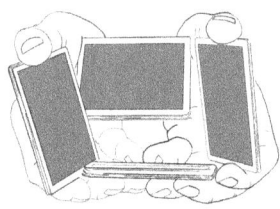 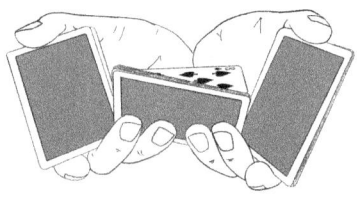

The 3rd and 4th fingers of both hands immediately curl inwards positioning their packet on top of the packet dropped between the palms, as in the first picture below. This creates the appearance of another three packet display, but it is important that the 3rd and 4th fingers do not release the grip of their packet.

The entire cut can also be neatly finished at this point with a nice easy close, where the 3rd and 4th fingers do release the grip on their packet and the side packets are pushed inwards, as in the second picture below. Also note that in the second picture below, the cards held between the hands are concealed behind the cards in front. A more complete description of this easy close can be found on page 33.

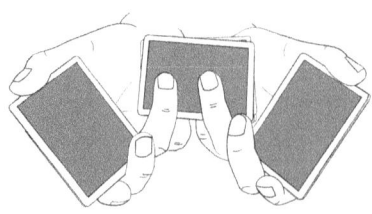 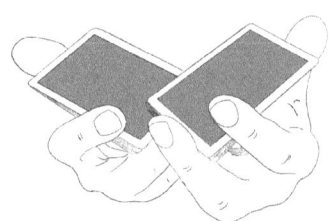

However, what actually happens next is that the outside packets, gripped between opposite short sides by the thumbs and the 1st and 2nd fingers, as in the first picture below, and as on the previous page, are re-gripped between the 1st finger tips on the outer long sides and the base of the thumbs at the packets' inner corners, as in the second picture below.

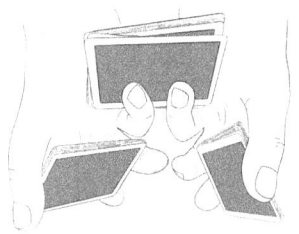 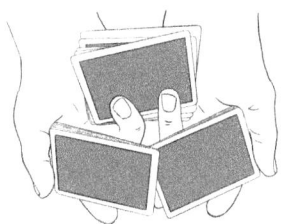

The 1st fingers move to the outer long edges of their packets. The 2nd fingers release their grip on the inner short edges and curl underneath as the thumbs press inwards. The 1st fingers slide down the outer long edges of their packets, regripping at the lower ends of these outer long edges. The inner corners of these packets drop down very slightly with the help of gravity and fall into place so as to be re-gripped by the base of the thumbs.

While the packets are gripped and squeezed between the 1st finger tips and the base of the thumbs, the tips of the thumbs push against the backs of the packets along the lower short edges, below the level of the 1st finger tips. This pivots the packets up vertically. The grip between the 1st finger tips and the base of the thumbs is not too tight so as to allow this hinging upwards movement.

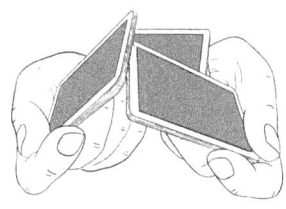

The hands also rotate very slightly at the wrist, the right hand clockwise and the left hand anti-clockwise, as if to turn the palms very slightly facing outwards. This also helps to raise up the outside packets.

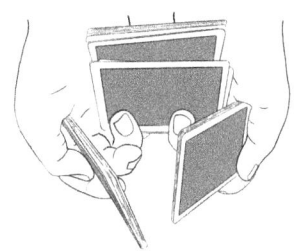 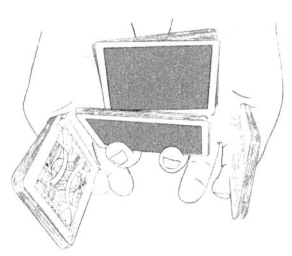

Once the outside packets are vertical, the pressure and grip between the base of the thumbs and tips of the 1st fingers is further loosened, allowing these packets to lean outwards to the sides, turning face up in the process. At the same time, the 3rd and 4th fingers of both hands uncurl, re-opening out their packet and turning it face up.

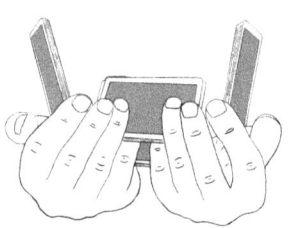 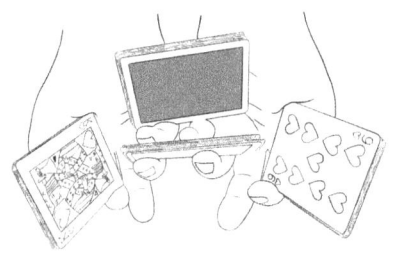

It is the loosening of the grip between the 1st fingers and base of the thumbs together with gravity which allows the outside packets to open and 'blossom' outwards. This process can also be assisted by continued pressure from the tips of the thumbs at the back of the packets, along the lower short edges, further helping the packets to pivot and fall outwards.

The face down packet which is just resting on the palms, can be gripped securely in place by the 2nd finger tips, by curling in the 2nd fingers, as in the second picture below. This also allows the hands to be tilted forward to give a better display of the cards.

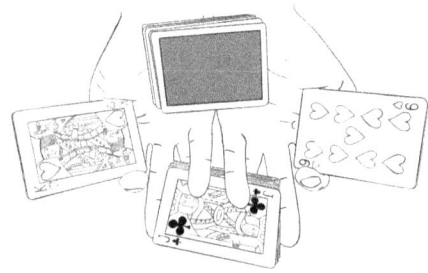 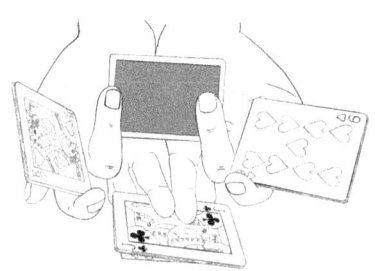

From here, the four packets can be very nicely and quickly closed, as in the picture to the right, completing the cut at this point. A more complete description of this quick close can be found on page 34.

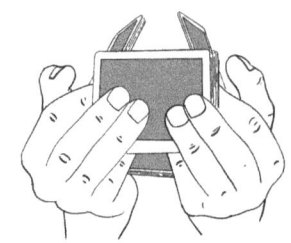

However, we have one more phase left in this kaleidoscopic, six packet display, exercise in concentration and dexterity… as follows.

The left 2nd finger relaxes its grip allowing the right 2nd finger to steal a single card from the top of its packet. The right 2nd finger presses down on the top of this packet and the right hand moves to the right, sliding the top card away with the card being gripped between the right 2nd finger-tip and the right palm, as in the first picture below.

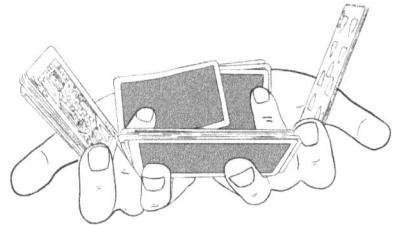 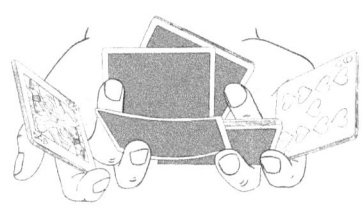

The palms separate allowing this single card 'packet' to be slid away. The packet remaining face down in the left palm is held in place by the left 2nd finger-tip.

In a like manner the left 3rd finger momentarily relaxes its grip allowing the right 3rd finger to steal away a single card from the top of its packet. This card is gripped between the right 3rd finger-tip and the back of the right 4th finger. The bulk of the packet remains clipped between the left 3rd finger-tip and the back of the left 4th finger, as in the second picture above.

The hands are separated creating another six packet display (two of the packets are in fact single cards). The hands can be held up palm outwards at face level, or alternatively the hands can be crossed over each other, as in the second picture below.

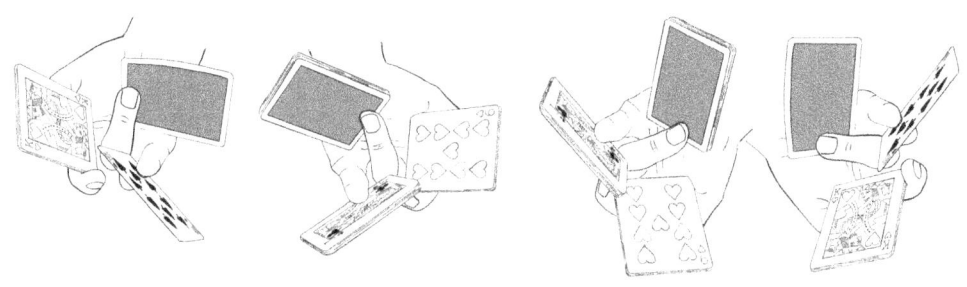

27

Further packets and displays can be created from this point…but for now we will head straight for the final close.

Thank you for following along up to this point. I sincerely hope it has been an enjoyable and inspiring experience and please feel welcome to create your own variations… I'm sure they would be fascinating to see.

The hands move back together and the packets are interlaced.

The packet held on the left palm is sandwiched between the two single cards of the right hand with the lower most single card being slid below this left hand's packet.

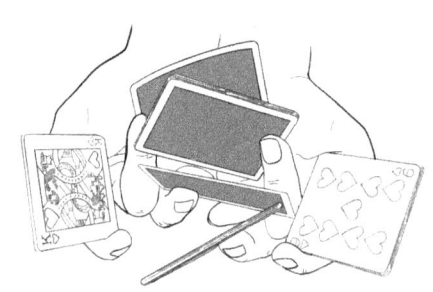

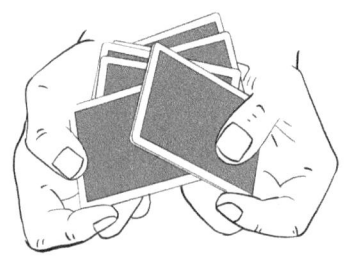

Next the left 3rd and 4th fingers are curled closing down their packet on top.

The right 2nd finger joins the left 3rd finger pressing down on top of the packet and aligning it with the packets below.

Finally, the two side packets gripped between the 1st fingers and base of the thumbs are allowed to fall and fold inwards and are placed down on top. It doesn't matter which side packet closes first, whichever feels more comfortable. The side packets are pressed down with the thumbs and the cards are squared up between the hands.

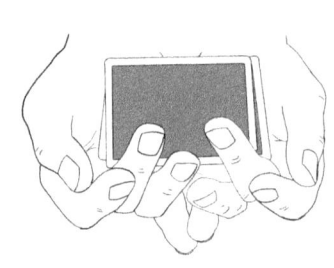

Basic scissor cut

Just for completeness, at this early point in the six packet display cut, as in the first picture below and as on page 19, scissor type cuts can be performed and completed as follows. (I hope there were enough 'as's in that sentence.) The thumbs continue moving upwards and outwards until the packets gripped between the thumbs and 1st fingers open out almost in line with the packets gripped between the 1st and 4th fingers.

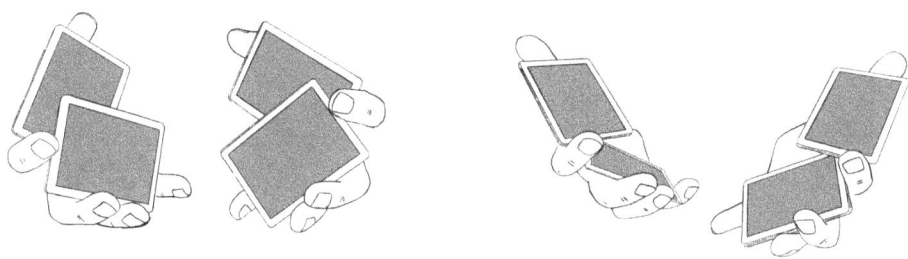

The inner corners of the packets gripped between the thumbs and 1st fingers gain clearance of the corners of the packets gripped between the 1st and 4th fingers. The 1st and 4th fingers widen their spread, loosening their grip, and allowing their packets to drop down onto the outstretched fingers. The thumbs move back in, pivoting in the new upper packets. These packets align with and are allowed to fall onto the packets below, the cards being straightened up in the hands with the 1st and 4th fingers at opposite short sides, and the thumbs and 2nd and 3rd fingers at opposite long sides.

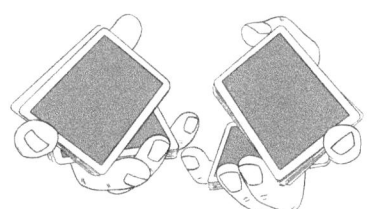
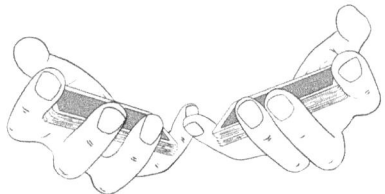

Variation on the three packet close

Once the pack has been arranged into a three packet line as in the first picture below, and as on page 22, there are several ways the cut can be completed with the cards being pivoted and zig-zagged closed. The 2nd and 3rd fingers press on the backs of their outside packets, aligning them with the packets directly behind them. The grip on the inner short edges of these outside packets is transferred from the 3rd and 4th fingers to the thumbs, resulting in one packet being held between the left 1st finger and thumb, a centre packet being held between the backs of the two thumbs and another outside packet being held between the right thumb and right 1st finger.

The 2nd and 4th fingers of both hands can help align the packets, if necessary, pressing and tapping them along the lower long edges, as in the second picture below. The 2nd fingers align the outside packets from below, and the 4th fingers can help align and straighten the centre packet.

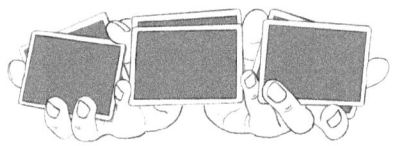 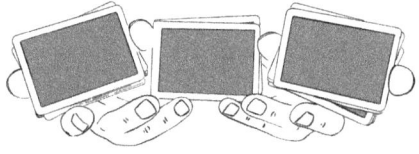

The 2nd, 3rd and 4th fingers of both hands are now free as in the first picture below, The right hand rotates clockwise and the left hand rotates anti-clockwise, revolving both outside packets so that they point downwards and at right angles to the centre packet.

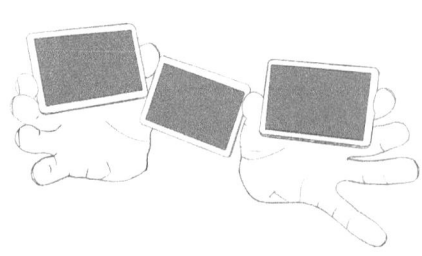 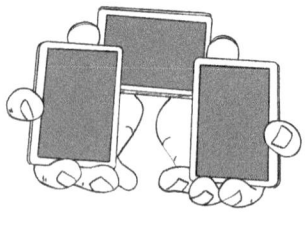

The hands continue to rotate, the right clockwise and the left anti-clockwise, turning the lower far short ends of their packets inwards, with the left hand packet overlapping the right packet, as in the first picture below, although note that it doesn't really matter which packet overlaps which, choose whichever feels more comfortable.

With a slight upward shake of the hands and releasing the pressure between the thumbs, the packet clipped between the thumbs is allowed drop down between the hands. The thumbs and fingers continue pushing their packets inwards, until they are aligned with the single packet held between the hands. The packets are aligned on top with the pack being squared up between the hands.

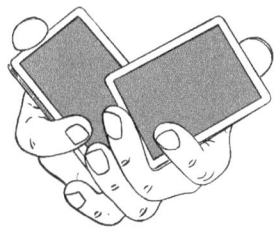

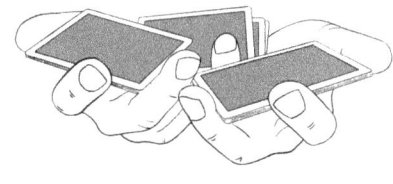

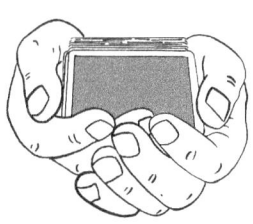

And if that wasn't enough fun, here's another version of this three packet close. Similar but different. This time, both hands rotate clockwise, resulting in the packets going into a zig-zag shape.

At the same time as the hands rotate, the 2nd and 3rd fingers move round onto the outer short sides of their packets and the 1st fingers move round onto the long sides of their packets. The 1st fingers press against the long sides, keeping them straight.

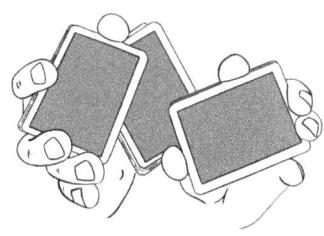

31

The hands continue to move together with the packet held between the left 1st finger and thumb moving in front of the centre packet. The right long edge of the centre packet presses against the right palm and the packet held between the right thumb and right 1st and 2nd fingers pivots in, in front of the other two packets. The fingers continue to align the three packets together and square up the cards in a vertical position.

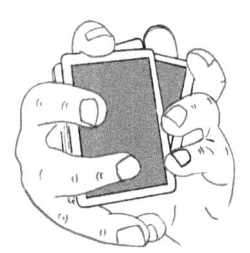

No end to the fun. And now, last but not least, here's another variation. You might think this variation is best, not because it is best but because it's last. This time, just the right hand on it's own rotates clockwise, pivoting in its packet, aligning it and joining it in front of the centre packet from underneath, as in the first picture below.

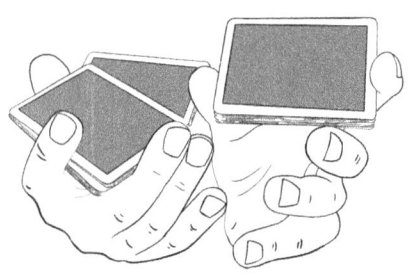 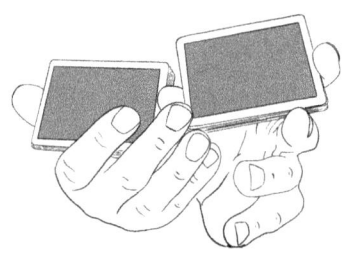

The left hand can now either rotate separately, again clockwise rotating its packet to join the other packets from over the top, depositing it in front of the two aligned packets in the right hand, as in the first picture below. Or the left hand can simply slide its packet across to the right pushing it with the fingers to align with and in front of the rest of the pack.

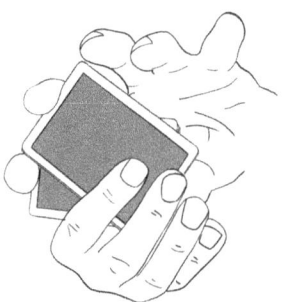 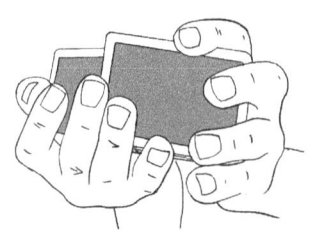

Easy Close

Once the phase has been reached as in the first picture below, and as on page 24, the entire display can be very neatly and easily closed. The 1st fingers move to the outside long edges of their packets, these two outside packets now being gripped at opposite short sides between the thumbs and 2nd fingers. These packets are pushed in towards each other by the thumbs, with the left hand's packet going over the top of the right hand's packet. Note that in the second picture below the two packets held between the hands are hidden behind the cards in front.

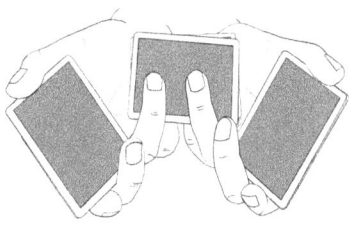
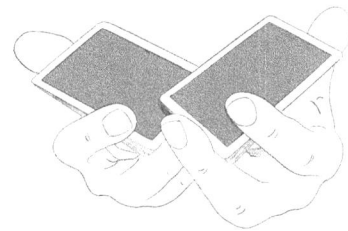

The 2nd fingers release their grip of the inner short edges of their packets. The thumbs continue pushing inwards. The left hand packet slides over the top of the right hand packet and the right hand packet slides over the back of the right 2nd finger tip.

The packets are aligned by a thumb on either short side and by the 1st fingers along the lower long side. The 2nd fingers and 3rd and 4th fingers uncurl, releasing their grip on their packets and leaving them in place. The packets are finally squared up from both sides and the front.

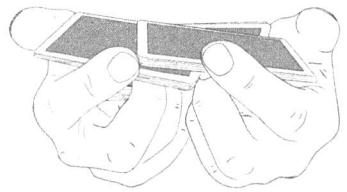
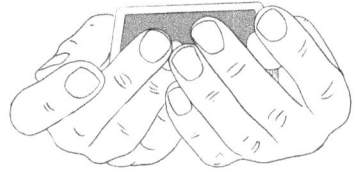

Quick Close

Once the phase has been reached as in the first picture below, and as on page 26, the entire display can be quickly and efficiently closed, with a reversing of the opening out of the outside packets. The left hand rotates very slightly clockwise and the right hand rotates very slightly anti-clockwise turning the palms inwards so as to slightly face each other. This action lifts back up the outside packets vertically. With a loosing of the grip between the 1st finger tips and the base of the thumbs, the outside packets are allowed to lean and fall inwards turning face down, They can also be tilted inwards and down by pushing with the tips of the thumbs. The packets are dropped onto and align with the face down packet resting between the hands. Again, it doesn't matter which side closes first, whichever seems more comfortable.

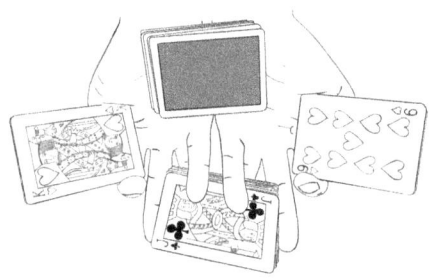 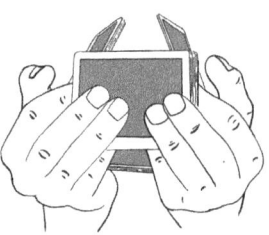

At the same time the 3rd and 4th fingers of both hands begin to curl, lifting their packet vertically. After the outside packets have been dropped, the 3rd and 4th fingers continue curling inwards, turning their packet face down on top of the packets resting between the palms, as in the pictures below. The 4th fingers are removed from beneath the top packet and the cards are squared up by both hands from the sides and the front.

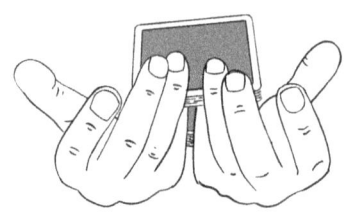 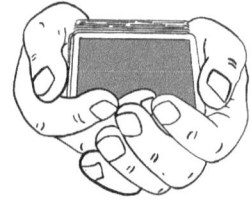

Further publications include

The Hinged Deck

Meditation for Magicians

The 52 Card Pick-up

Further information at

www.cardflourish.co.uk

www.balloonanimal.co.uk

Published by Balloon Animal

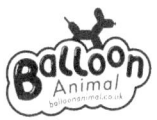